MY ETIQUETTE SOURCE

MY ETIQUETTE SOURCE

CE Lee and Trudy Redus

authorHOUSE®

AuthorHouse™
1663 Liberty Drive
Bloomington, IN 47403
www.authorhouse.com
Phone: 1-800-839-8640

© 2015 CE Lee and Trudy Redus. All rights reserved.

No part of this book may be reproduced, stored in a retrieval system, or transmitted by any means without the written permission of the author.

Published by AuthorHouse   03/06/2015

ISBN: 978-1-4918-4657-5 (sc)

Print information available on the last page

Any people depicted in stock imagery provided by Thinkstock are models, and such images are being used for illustrative purposes only. Certain stock imagery © Thinkstock.

This book is printed on acid-free paper.

Because of the dynamic nature of the Internet, any web addresses or links contained in this book may have changed since publication and may no longer be valid. The views expressed in this work are solely those of the author and do not necessarily reflect the views of the publisher, and the publisher hereby disclaims any responsibility for them.

Contents

Acknowledgment ix
Introduction xi

<u>Chapter 1</u>
The Difference between Respect and Manners.............. 1
What is Respect?... 1
What is Etiquette?... 1
What are Manners?... 2

<u>Chapter 2</u>
First Impressions... 5
The Twelve-Inch Rule: 12-12-12-12-24 for First
Impressions 6
You Are Being Judged 6

<u>Chapter 3</u>
The Best Handshake 9

<u>Chapter 4</u>
Introductions – The Six Sisters of Introduction 11

<u>Chapter 5</u>
Magic Words 16
Polite Conversation—Meet and Greet 17

<u>Chapter 6</u>
Networking – 19

<u>Chapter 7</u>
Telephone and Cell Phone Etiquette 25

<u>Chapter 8</u>
Intergeneration 29

<u>Chapter 9</u>
Prom Etiquette - Tips for the Prom or other Special
Event 31

<u>Chapter 10</u>
Dining Etiquette 33
Understanding the Table Setting 33

<u>Chapter 11</u>
American and Continental/European Styles of Dining.... 44

<u>Chapter 12</u>
Bread, Soup, Broth/Bouillon... 53

<u>Chapter 13</u>
Tea, Coffee, Desserts - Cups and Saucers.................... 56

<u>Chapter 14</u>
Toasts 59

<u>Chapter 15</u>
Business Dining, Social Dining and Tipping............... 61

Chapter 16
General Etiquette Guidelines 66
Table spills, elbows and everything else 66
General Etiquette Guidelines 68

Chapter 17
Difficult Foods 69

Chapter 18
Guidelines for Confident Dining 71
Thank you and Goodbye 73

Chapter 19
Foreign and Other Words Found on Menus 75

Chapter 20
My Mini Etiquette Dictionary 81

About Us 103
About the Authors 105
About the Book 107

www.etiquetteliny.com

Acknowledgment

Dear_____:

Thank you for the wonderful luncheon on business etiquette at Baruch College.

I attended first grade in another country, and our first lesson was on dining etiquette. I feel that knowing proper etiquette is very important, and it is highly overlooked in our schools today (along with grammar lessons). However, I am glad to see that experts like you are changing that. I learned a tremendous amount during the luncheon on March 22, and I apply these skills every day.

Thank you once more.

Lilya

Introduction

Our vision is of a world filled with individuals who conduct business and social activities with confidence, respect and dignity. The golden rule is to treat others as you would like to be treated. This is how we have chosen to live our lives and we hope that you will join us.

My Etiquette Source is a concise and clear guide to social skills necessary to thrive and survive successfully in today's diverse society—at home, away from home, at work, or at play. This guidebook incorporates features pertaining to meetings, greetings, and dining skills where business and social interaction are conducted.

My Etiquette Source is an invaluable reference guide. It is designed not to intimidate, but to encourage those who wish to enhance their comfort level and social skills. Information was gathered and tested through real life experiences, guaranteed to make a difference in your life and pique your interest. We hope you will build on this opportunity by jotting notes and collecting tips, and one day soon, you would be able to update your own version—"My Etiquette Tips." Practice, practice, practice. Consistency is the key. It takes 21 days to start a new pattern.

It is the writer's hope that the material contained will assist with the development of confidence and social interaction.

"Books are the quietest and most constant of friends; they are the most accessible and wisest of counselors, and the most patient of teachers".

~ Charles W. Eliot

Chapter 1

The Difference between Respect and Manners

Aretha Franklin sang the song, "R-E-S-P-E-C-T."

What is Respect?

It comes from within and embodies the human heart. Manners are taught as proper social education. Respect is earned by holding your behavior and expectations at a high moral level. Respect does not occur because you have manners, but manners, as part of good behavior, are developed because you are a respectful person. *We earn respect through positive behavior; it is an attitude and way of life.* **RESPECT IS EARNED.**

What is Etiquette?

Etiquette is originally a French word meaning "ticket" or little signs, translated and interpreted as rules for social and professional interaction. It has specific rules and guidelines for socially acceptable behavior and building relationships. Over the years many of the rules were modified to become more adaptable for usage in modern society. However, showing consideration for others and basic decency, never went out of style. – "The golden rule is still alive and doing fine."

When etiquette skills are developed, like tools handled by a skilled professional, you would know, how, when and why certain actions and reactions are appropriate and will use them to assist in determining your future success.

Quick Tips:

- Be sensitive to the feelings of others and think before you speak.
- Be attentive when someone is speaking.
- Be polite, considerate, and understanding.
- Admit to errors and do not hesitate to apologize for short comings.
- Be on time and let your word be your bond.
- Be dependable and trustworthy.

Show respect for yourself and others you encounter daily, with special attention to your elders, professors, veterans, and individuals who have made positive contributions to society. All of their positive efforts have resulted in making it easier for people to live together as a community and in the world.

What are Manners?

Manners lead us back to the old saying of treating others the way you would like to be treated. This has an impact on how you are seen and respected by others. Manners, linked to the rules of etiquette, are practiced daily through social interactions. When you are nice to someone, showing consideration and respect, there is a 98 percent chance that they would be nice to you.

- ♦ Use the Magic Words - Please, Thank you, Excuse me and I am Sorry, these are just a few, with "I am sorry" being the most difficult.
- ♦ Instead of trying to avoid eye contact, greet others "Good morning or Good afternoon."
- ♦ Holding the door open when hands are full.
- ♦ Remembering to say 'Thank you' to someone who gave you something or did you a favor.
- ♦ Be patient when waiting in line or waiting to be served.
- ♦ Rise above derogatory situations.

Manners are a rare commodity in today's society, use it to stand out in the crowd and influence others. When scores are equal, decisions are made on that rare quality "Something about that individual that cannot be defined". Most often it is manners - being respectful, polite, compassionate and confident. It is how you make the other person feel.

Good manners are free as the wind yet extremely effective in providing opportunities to excel and create the competitive edge. Start at home by treating loved ones with respect and dignity, and then let this practice flow into daily interactions with others at school, work, and play.

Manners and respect reflect not only what we say and feel about others but also how we feel about ourselves.

"Really great people make you feel that you too can become great"

~ Mark Twain

Chapter 2

First Impressions

When entering a room, always try to make a good impression, because you rarely get a second chance to make a good *First Impression*. It takes 5 seconds to make an impression. Once the first impression is made it is virtually irreversible.

- Before you leave home- Get to know and use your mirror—*it is your best friend.*
- Smile - Enter with poise, purpose and confidence, head up shoulders back.
- Make eye contact with others as you discreetly survey the room.
- Greet others graciously.

In this book reference is constantly being made to the Golden Rule - (Treat others the way you would like to be treated). The basic school ruler is 12 inches – so why not make the association in order to remember the basic facts.

The Twelve-Inch Rule: 12-12-12-12-24 for First Impressions

- ♦ The first 12 steps as you enter the room enter with confidence.
- ♦ The first 12 words – make them positive and meaningful.
- ♦ The first 12 inches from the tip of your head to your neck - be sure you are well groomed - hair, eyebrows, nose, lips and make-up.
- ♦ The last - 12 inches from your feet up - shoes, socks or stockings, if bare feet - toes clean and heels smooth.
- ♦ 12+12 = 24 Seconds to make an impression

"He was a bold man who first ate an oyster"
~ Jonathan Swift

You Are Being Judged

It may not be fair, but a person's first judgment of you is based on your appearance. When people look at you, they make judgments based on what they see. We are a visual culture, unless you are visually impaired, we all make these evaluations in business and social environments. Your appearance creates a picture of who you are. Unfortunately, people may use your personal appearance to judge your character.

The three second rule works like this:

- If you appear to be of comparable business or social level, you are considered suitable for further interaction.
- If you appear to be of higher business or social status, you are admired and cultivated as a valuable contact.
- If you appear to be of lower business or social standing, you are tolerated but kept at arm's length.
- If you are in an interview situation, you can either appear to match the corporate culture or not, ultimately affecting the outcome.

Your appearance is a symbolic statement of who you are. It speaks volumes, before you say a single word.

Opinions are made from the moment you enter the presence of a group or even encounter an individual.

You will realize that you never get a second chance to make a first impression. More often, you are immediately judged based on any one or more of the following criteria.

Read going down each column for example – Appearance – Gender, color of skin ……………….

Appearance	Diction	Socioeconomic Status	Ethnic Background	Mannerism	Attitude
Gender	Enunciation	Job Status	Race	Body language	Positive
Color of Skin	Accent	Rich	Country of origin	Distinctive way of walking & talking	Negative
Approachability	Colloquial	Poor	Language	Unique writing style	Indifferent
Attitude	Slang	Middle Class	Dress Code	Tapping of feet	Confident
Age	Pronunciation	Occupation	Culture	Toss of hair or head	Sarcastic
Attractiveness	Voice quality	Education	Religion	Biting nails	Respectful
Weight	Grammar	Neighborhood	Ancestry	Special way of greeting	Aggressive
Grooming	Inflection	Political power	Beliefs	Gestures	Loving

"First impressions are important, but everyone deserves a second chance." ~ Unknown

Chapter 3

The Best Handshake

The handshake is the first personal contact between individuals for proper social and business meeting introductions.

Quick Tips:

- Be sure that your hands are clean, dry and warm. Smile, make eye contact, then extend your right hand, thumb slightly apart, connect web to web and make a firm handshake.
- Ladies can remain seated during introductions. However, if the person to whom she is being introduced is older or a figure of authority she should stand, if possible.
- Men should stand to shake hands when introduced. Wait for a lady to extend her hand before shaking

(do not grab). When shaking her hand, be gentle, avoid a crushing handshake.
- If someone introduces you to another whose arm is in a cast or is amputated, you should extend your hand and let the person shake it with the left hand, salute or use their preferred greeting acknowledgement.

When you feel that you may be exposed to any germs, unsanitary conditions or are not comfortable shaking hands, it is acceptable to smile or nod your head, bow, do the fist bump, salute for a handshake, or even create your own acceptable signal.

"Friendship is composed of a single soul inhabiting two bodies"

~ Aristotle

Chapter 4

Introductions – The Six Sisters of Introduction

In business and social settings introductions are important when meeting someone for the first time or when you recognize someone but they do not remember you. Make them feel welcome, by introducing yourself, it is a positive gesture, that helps to put people at ease.

- Stand – when you meet someone for the first time. You should also stand to greet someone if that person is standing.
- See their eyes – make eye contact when speaking (practice at home in front of the mirror).
- Smile – a smile is the same in any language.
- Shake hands – extend your right hand and use your whole hand, thumb slightly apart to connect web to web. Do not grab too tightly or shake more than three or four times.
- Say – Greetings with their names.
- Say – Response including the person's name.

Formal Introductions

Begin introductions by using the pecking order of the highest ranking official to those of a lower position. Persons of lesser authority are introduced to persons of greater authority regardless of gender.

"Mr. General Manager I would like to introduce, Mary Green the clerk from the stock room."

(Do not use "You to") it reverses the order.

"Mr. General Manager I would like to introduce to you Mr. Jones, reporter for the Herald News."

Introduce the older person to the younger person. That is, the first name spoken should be that of the older person Give the first and last name when possible.

Example – When introducing your grandmother to a friend, turn to your grandma and say, "Grandma, this is my friend from school, Andrew Adams."

Turn to Andrew and say, "Andrew this is my grandma, Mrs. Jones."

Example – When introducing a sibling to a friend.

"Mary Jones I would like to introduce, Kendall, my brother."

Example – When introducing a friend to your parents (honored).

Turn to your parent and say, "I would like to introduce Tommy Jones to you. He is in my art class."

Tommy replies, "Hello, it is nice to meet you, Mr. Lee."

When introducing your parent to your teacher (honored). "Mrs. Jones, I would like to introduce my mother, Janette Abreu" (or Mrs. Abreu).

Parent: "Mrs. Jones, it is a pleasure to meet you."

Informal Introductions

Begin by saying your name – "Hello, my name is Gabbie Williams" The person then replies, "Hello, I am DeAnna Lee. It is nice to meet you."

Gabbie should respond with – "It is nice to meet you too, DeAnna."

Be consistent during informal group introductions, either use the full names, or add a title as needed. Example - "Mary Jones I want to introduce Kristin Lam" or "Miss Jones I want to introduce Miss Lam." If there is a mixed gender group and they are about the same age mention the names of females first.

In professional settings introductions are more formal use complete names and titles.

"The very essence of politeness is to take care that by our words and actions we make other people pleased with us as well as with themselves. ~ Jean de La Brugere

Group Introductions

Host/hostess should always rise to greet each arriving guest.

- Group introductions, during informal affairs introduce the new person and request that the others introduce themselves. Keep checking to ensure that everyone was introduced.
- Remember the Six Sisters: Stand, See, Smile Shake, Speak, and the other person will Say your name.

Quick Tips:

- When someone has a title always use it.
- Stand when you meet someone, unless you are in an inconvenient seating position.
- During introductions additional information about the person, such as where they are from, their hobbies and interests goes a long way. This gives people something to work with and continues the conversation.

- When asked how are you? Respond with "I am fine thank you, how are you? or "Thank you for asking, I am doing fine."
- Avoid "I am doing good" - "Fine or Ok." Definitely, do not respond by listing your afflictions and problems.
- Avoid or minimize gestures.
- Always seek the opportunity to introduce yourself, it reflects confidence and authority.
- If during introductions your name is mispronounced or any information is incorrect, make immediate corrections in a friendly manner.

"Be sincere, be brief, be seated." ~ Franklin Roosevelt

Chapter 5

Magic Words

Remember to use the Magic Words and use them often: They can open doors, and build respect.

- Good morning
- Good evening
- Goodnight
- May I – May I please
- Please - Yes please
- Thank you
- No thank you
- Yes, thank you
- You are welcome
- Excuse me
- I am sorry
- Goodbye

Quick Tips:

Avoid using slangs "My bad" - - Yeah, naah, What's Up! How you doing? especially in formal settings. Instead use "I am sorry", "Pardon me "and" How are you?"

"Good manners and respect never fail" ~ *Author*

Polite Conversation—Meet and Greet

Do you ever wish you could disappear instead of starting or joining a conversation?

Here are some guidelines to help you handle most conversations -

- Practice interacting and speaking informally, example – at the dining table.
- Sit (if possible) and speak with several guests for at least five to ten minutes, and listen.
- Remember, the hearing and speech impaired. Make eye contact and try some sign language if needed, also speak slowly.
- Each interaction is special. It is what you say and do and how you make others feel.

Some appropriate topics for polite social conversation

- Speak quietly, but do not mumble.
- Know your audience and adjust your conversation accordingly.
- Be knowledgeable about several topics and discuss common topics. Local newspaper articles, positive news, entertainment, books, hobbies, weather, art, music, sports, holidays.
- Your plans and dreams that you feel are not private (if asked).
- Listen attentively and learn, comment, ask open-ended questions, and give others an opportunity to speak. It is not all about you.

Avoid the following:

- Taboo or controversial subjects such as - money, religion, politics, personal appearance, terminal illness and private family situations.
- Arrogant, lectures and talking down to the listener.
- Talking endlessly about your job, especially at workplace events.
- Do not take over the conversation, exaggerate experiences, or try to impress with lies or delusions of grandeur. Remember you cannot hide the truth.

"If you cannot say anything positive about someone, say nothing"

~ Unknown

Chapter 6

Networking –

Networking is building relationships that are mutually beneficial.

To exceed within a group takes work. Imagine being able to stand out from the crowd as being a polished professional and also a much appreciated co-worker or companion. This combination gives you the edge to make an outstanding impression. You feel confident, self assured and optimistic. This comes from practice, it comes from understanding and applying the total business package. It is a skill that could be learned.

Someone with great grades, impressive athletic performance, but a shy loner, reluctant to speak-up and interact is not necessarily who companies are pursuing for leadership positions. Why? Corporate America or any business is looking for a total package to represent them. What skills will you bring to the table?

Just like going to the gift wrapping section of a department store and requesting that a gift be wrapped for a special occasion. Immediately, you are attracted to the one with the most exquisite and impeccable wrapping - rich paper, ribbons, streamers and card. It may be expensive, but definitely worth taking a second look. Likewise, standout from the crowd in a positive manner and you will gain acknowledgement and consideration.

Successful people network for various reasons. Career or business networking is an excellent tool for finding and landing your next great opportunity.

According to the Wall Street Journal 94% of new job finders cited networking as their primary mode of job search.

Networking required skills

Be Prepared
Arrive on time with a plan – What are my intentions and what do I intend to achieve.

Introductions
Always stand. Smile. Firm hand shake. Eye-to-eye contact. Say your first and last name. Wear your name-tag on your upper right side. It is easier for others to read during conversations.

Body Language
Making a good impression includes your body language. Start with posture - standing erect with shoulders back and make eye contact, if you find this overbearing then focus on the person's eyebrows instead of eyes. Do not mumble, voice and diction are extremely important.

Fidgeting - do not play with your hair, eyes, etc., that includes constantly checking your cell phone, this is a sign of nervousness, anxiety or lack of interest. If you are nervous take deep breaths, and visualize a calm setting, such as the beach.

Avoid touching other people during a conversation, give them space.

Remember to pause and listen. Give others an opportunity to express their interests. No one ever learns anything while they are talking.

A handshake alone is professional. (Hands can be washed or sanitized discretely).

Today due to health concerns some people avoid handshakes, especially in social settings and prefer to use the fist bump. Should this happen do not feel offended. Do not be surprised if very soon the fist bump becomes acceptable in professional settings.

Mixing and Mingling - Enter the room with confidence and purpose then introduce yourself.

Engage in polite conversation for a few minutes, close conversation and circulate.

Ask open-ended questions, this helps to keep the conversation moving.

If refreshments are served, hold your beverage in your left hand. This leaves your right hand dry and warm for a proper handshake.

Have your crisp business cards ready. A case will keep them in good condition. Please use your discretion when distributing your business cards. Never distribute a dirty or damaged business card.

Additional benefits of networking

- ♦ Personal connections are the primary factor that most often leads to getting ahead.
- ♦ Networking groups are an excellent source of information and ideas about events, trends, opportunities and industry news. You can also find support for your proposals and the chance to help others.
- ♦ Charitable fundraising is also driven heavily by personal and professional networking.
- ♦ Relationships – with potential and existing clients and vendors. People prefer to conduct and refer business to people they know and trust.
- ♦ Very important to Listen and Learn.

Correspondence

Email etiquette and other correspondence

- ♦ Be timely with all responses and correspondence.
- ♦ Have a relevant subject line, you may want your recipient to refer to your email.

- Pay attention to spelling and grammar. 'Spell check' is not fool proof.
- Proofreading carefully and with another pair of eyes is still in style.
- Errors can result in loss of credibility.
- Customers or clients send emails because they want a quick response, sometimes immediately, but at least within twenty four hours or less. If the reply requires research or investigation, send a quick response, or make a phone call stating that you received their email and will contact them with updated relevant information as soon as possible.
- Answer all questions. An unanswered question is a waste of time. Rest assured you will get another email regarding those unanswered questions.
- Do not convey feelings of anger, watch your tone, keep flaming under control and minimize usage of "flag" or symbols.
- Emails are not private; they can be saved, copied, forwarded and used against you.

Other Correspondence

- Be timely. Use quality paper. Make the envelope professional as well. Thank you notes should be sent within 24 hours.
- Social media is being done by everyone. If you do, be sure that the information is what you want to share with the world.

Remembering your networking requirements - <u>N-A-M-E-S</u>

N- NAMES - Remember and pronounce them correctly
A-ACCOMPLISHMENTS   - Address with confidence
M-MENTOR   - Find and adopt one
E- EXPERTISE   - Exhibit them
S- SKILLS   - Market them

" Do not follow the path, go where there is no path to begin your trail" ~ Ashanti Proverb

Chapter 7

Telephone and Cell Phone Etiquette

Ring, ring, ring. Some find this a sign of potential business or social opportunity, while others a source of annoyance.

Placing phone calls from home

Before you pick up the phone, pick up your watch, or look at the clock, ask yourself. "Is this a good time to call?" Will you be interrupting anyone? Do you have something important to say? Think before you call.

- Let the person who answers the telephone know who is calling. ("Hello, this is Gabbie. May I speak with DeAnna, please?").
- Do not speak loudly, scream nor make crank calls.
- Remember to say please and thank you when you ask for your friend.
- If someone you recognize answers the phone, greet that person politely. ("How are you today, Mr. Jones?").

- If the person is not there, ask to leave a message or say you will call back.
- If this is a business related call, get the name of the person who is taking the message.
- Ask permission before putting someone on speakerphone and be considerate of others in the surrounding area.
- Let the person at the other end of the phone know when you are putting him or her on hold, especially when a cell phone is used.
- Thank the person and say goodbye before you quietly hang up.

Receiving phone calls at home

Should someone call your home, take the call politely without giving out too much personal information.

- Answer the phone as clearly as possible, the way your parents requested, or just a polite "Hello". If you realize that the call is not intended for you, and a specific person was requested, get them to the phone promptly.
- When the person is home, tell the caller, "Just a minute, please," or "Please wait while I get the person requested." "May I tell (him/her) who is calling?" When looking for the person who was called, do not drop the phone and shout his or her name. Put the phone on hold, call the person quietly, and make sure not to disturb someone if he or she is sleeping, unless it is an emergency. Remember to get back to the phone quickly and not leave the caller on hold, nor the line open.

My Etiquette Source

- If the person cannot come to the phone, indicate that the person can't come to the phone right now. Ask the caller, " May I take a message and have Mom call you later?" Do not tell the caller what the person is doing!
- If you are alone, it is best to keep that information private. Simply say, "They cannot come to the phone right now. May I have them call you?"

Phone calls at work

- When answering phones at work you are representing your company and yourself. Put a smile on your face before you pickup, as people on the other end can "see your smile in your voice."
- Answer the phone promptly. Be courteous and professional, speak clearly and at a moderate rate. The person on the other end can detect your mood, tone and accent. Sometimes they would ask – "Where are you located? Are you out of state, or out of the country?"
- Minimize distraction, during the conversation, it can be detected by your tone, as if you are trying to rush the caller off the line.
- Notify, or ask permission before you put the caller on hold or on the speaker phone. If the hold is for a long time, keep checking in.
- Take detailed messages - Name, contact information- phone and e-mail.
- Do not share company messages with co-workers.
- Check answering machine for messages and respond as needed.

Cell phones, text messaging, and other forms of electronic communications

Be considerate and thoughtful when and where you use electronic devices.

- Put your phone on vibrate if you are in a public place - church, restaurant, theatre, library, concert classroom, or when entering someone's home to have a private conversation. Notify your guest if you are expecting a call.
- Return phone calls at the end of meetings, or as soon as possible.
- Excuse yourself if you have to accept an urgent call.
- Avoid lengthy ring tones and songs. You may be missing an important call or message in an emergency.
- Avoid lengthy conversations, especially in public places. Politely shorten the conversation and return the call later.

Chapter 8

Intergeneration

It is proven that every twenty-five years a new generation begins. Consequently, it is not surprising to experience interactions with one generation in elementary school, another in college, some in the workforce and others retired. In some programs it is very common to see teenagers assisting seniors with their cell phones and computers. To encourage the interaction it is important that we learn how to effectively deal with this situation.

Here are some hints:

- Always honor and respect your elders.
- Do not make older people feel uncomfortable because of failing senses such as hearing and eyesight – Instead, make them feel relevant and recognize wisdom.
- Do not ignore or make fun of older people.
- Speak slowly and clearly.
- Avoid off-color jokes.

- Avoid being too familiar. Use titles such as Mr. Mrs., Dr., etc.
- Do not comment about a scent of perfume, odor, or clothes.
- Do not touch or move any objects from their original placement.
- Offer your seat, offer to help, and use your best manners.
- Be polite.
- Be patient when seniors ask for assistance with their electronic devices.
- In general, when an offer to assist in any form is rejected, do not keep insisting.

"Today it is necessary to behave as if you are being watched recorded and/or photographed. Yesterday, it was always behave as if you are being watched." ~ Author

Chapter 9

Prom Etiquette - Tips for the Prom or other Special Event

Do you have a date for the prom? Although many people now go in groups or by themselves. Prom is still a big event, especially for girls.

Quick Tips:

- ♦ Ladies should be asked three weeks prior, to have ample time to find a dress. If you accept an invitation you are committed. You cannot sit around waiting on a better offer that may or may not come.
- ♦ The name of the game is planning. Some companies offer discounts for those who plan ahead. Contact local vendors, restaurants, limousine services, tuxedo rentals etc. for early bird discounts.
- ♦ It is not uncommon for couples or groups to share the costs. As soon as you decide to go, talk about the cost and decide how to share it. Most couples or groups split everything equally. Including tickets,

transportation and meal. Be sure to include the tip if not already included in the service.
- When it comes to flowers, we are often clueless as to what works in the color family. Your date is wearing his or her favorite color "chartreuse". White goes with everything. If you are lucky to receive a corsage or boutonniere, please wear it!
- Formal attire still means tuxedos and long gowns. Semi-formal is for short dresses and jackets (dinner jackets or sport coats) with neckties. You are looking your best so mind your manners and don't forget to take pictures that will make you proud, many years later.
- If you are going to the prom, you are going to have a great time so dance, everybody dances at the prom, whether you are solo or with a group.
- Don't forget curfew! If you are running late or plans change, call your parents.

One final thought, please do not text and drive nor drink and drive. Do not get into the car with anyone who has been drinking excessively. Better yet, take the keys away from the driver, if possible, and call a taxi or your parents. They will still be awake. Prom night should be filled with happy memories for everyone.

" Every action done in company ought to be with some sign of respect, to those that are present". ~ George Washington

Chapter 10

Dining Etiquette

Understanding the Table Setting

Try to remember what your mother always said, "Elbows off the table and sit up straight."

From the time you were old enough, you were helping to set the table. Take the silverware, place the napkins. There was something for us all to do when it came to setting the table for a meal. Lucky for us, some of the rigid formal dinner requirements of days past has changed, but dining skills remain very important today especially in social and professional settings.

American Style - Four Course Setting

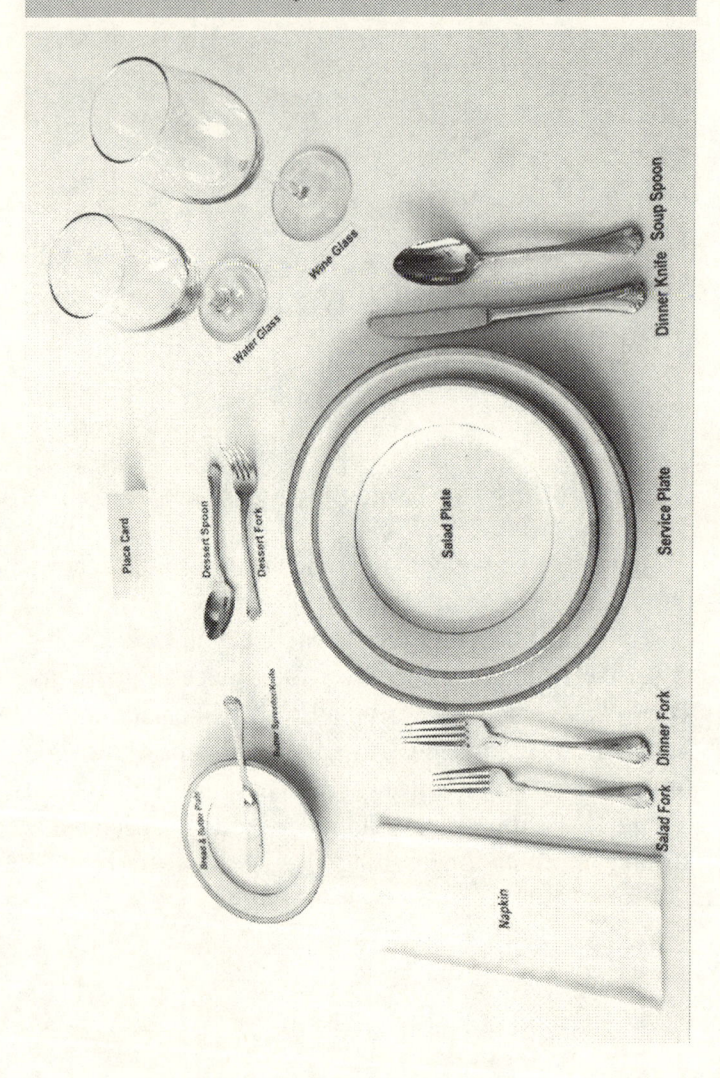

American Style - Diagram 1

My Etiquette Source

However complicated this sea of dishes, glasses, and utensils appears to you do not panic. You can familiarize yourself with it by drawing a quick and easy imaginary vertical line down the center of the main service plate. Remember to use utensils from the outside moving inwards towards the plate.

To the left of this line is the napkin, above is the bread and butter plate with butter spreader/knife. Lower left is the salad fork and dinner fork.

(Fish knife, fork and salad knife not shown in this four course setting)

Fish knife and fork are placed in order of use based on entree or appetizer. If fish is the main course the fish fork is placed to the left of the plate and fish knife will be right of the plate. When fish is served as an appetizer the fish knife is placed to the right of the dinner knife and the fish fork to the left of the dinner fork.

To the right is a dinner or service knife and soup spoon. Upper right water glass/goblet and wine glass.

Salad plate or Soup bowl placed on the service plate.

The red wine glass is slightly wider than the white wine glass. (Champagne glass not shown the flute shaped glass is for champagne and is often brought to the table if needed for a toast. Teacup, saucer and teaspoon provided as needed).

The "charger plate/service plate" is the largest, sometimes an ornate plate, placed in the center of the setting. In some cases, it is used like a place holder and will be removed before the first course is served otherwise it is used like a place mat for the earlier courses and will be removed before the main meal is served.

The dessert utensils, usually consisting of a dessert spoon and a cake fork, located directly above the service plate.

Salad plate or Soup bowl is located on top of the service plate, or brought out separately.

(Knives forks and spoons sometimes referred to as cutlery, flatware or silverware)

Note: Continental setting, the salad fork is *after the dinner fork. American setting the salad fork will be before the dinner fork, as Americans eat salad first.*

My Etiquette Source

Continental/European Style - Four Course Setting

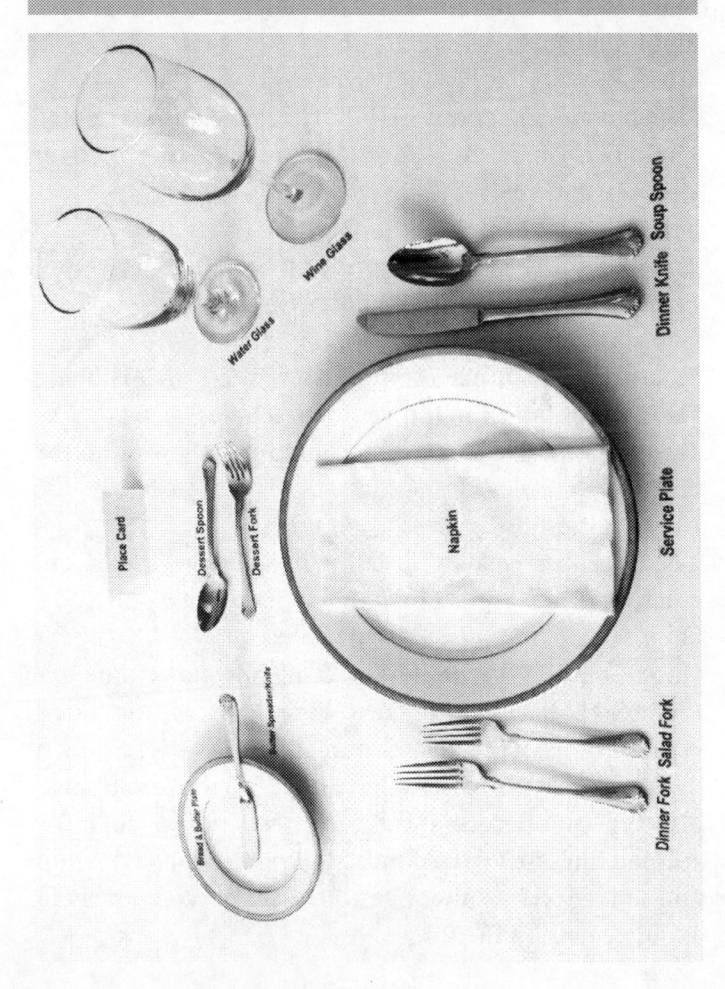

Draw a quick and easy imaginary vertical line down the center of the main service plate.

To the upper left of this line is the bread and butter plate with butter knife/spreader, lower left Dinner fork and Salad fork.

If fish is being served Fish Fork, Dinner Fork, Salad Fork. (Fish knife and fork , salad fork and appetizer fork not shown).

To the right is a Dinner knife and Soup spoon. Upper right, Water glass/goblet and Wine glass.

Salad Knife, Dinner Knife, Fish Knife if fish is being served. Seafood Fork if seafood is being served. The seafood/appetizer fork is the only fork allowed on the right.

The dessert utensils, consisting of a dessert spoon and a dessert fork, are located above the service plate.

Note: Reading these table settings preparations are made for a four course meal. Five or six course meals require more wine glasses and silverware. Not shown in these settings are the salad knife, fish knife and fork, also the appetizer/seafood fork, the smallest fork for seafood like shrimp cocktails. Teaspoon, along with cup and saucer for tea or coffee - often served separately to avoid crowding the table.

The Silverware/Flatware/Cutlery:

Forks: Forks and spoons on the right of the plate. The exception to this is the cake fork which is located directly above the plate with its handle pointing in the

My Etiquette Source

direction of the other forks. A fish fork is placed if a six-course meal is being served. **The dinner fork is the largest of the three forks, the salad fork is the smallest. Its position relative to the dinner fork depends on the dining style implemented. In the American style of dining, salad is served prior to the main course, in which case, the salad fork is placed to the left of the dinner fork. (See American Style diagram) Not included, is the appetizer fork, which is the smallest of all forks. In the European style of dining, salad is served after the main course, in which case, the salad fork is placed to the right of the dinner fork.** When a fork is used alone for eating, it is held in the right hand with tines pointing up. The handle of the fork rests on the middle finger, supported by the outer two fingers. The spoon used alone should be held in the right hand like a fork.

Appetizer fork

Holding the dinner or salad fork

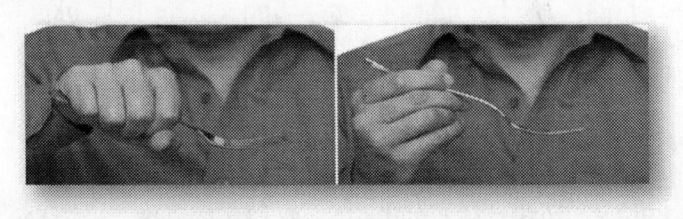

Never   Always

Holding the spoon

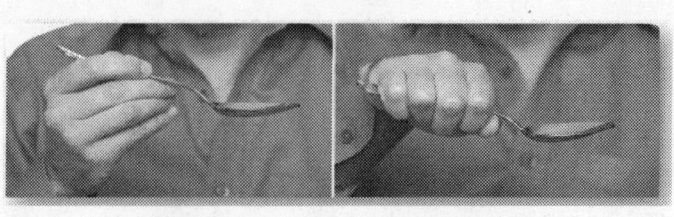

Always   *Never*

Knives: Place the knives to the right of the service plate. The exception to this is the butter knife, which is placed horizontally across the top of the bread and butter plate, its handle pointing in the direction of the other knives.

Spoons: Unlike forks and knives, spoons are minimal on the table setting. In this case, there are three (refer to diagram1 page 34 - American Style). The dessert spoon is placed directly above the service plate, its handle pointing in the direction of the soup spoon. The soup spoon, next to the teaspoon is the larger of the two spoons and is placed to the right of the knives.

In settings, when the tea or coffee cup are not included, teaspoons are brought out later. Spoons are held like a fork. Sip from the side of the spoon.

The Glassware:

Non stemmed - Drinking glasses, tumblers, bar glasses, plates, cups and bowls.

Based upon the occasion, glasses may be placed as needed throughout the meal.

My Etiquette Source

Water glass – Stemmed or usually non-stemmed glasses used for water, place setting on the right.

White wine glass-Stemware- glass with a narrow bowl that rests on a stem, attached to a base or foot for balance

Red wine glass- Stemware – glass with a wider bowl than that of a white wine glass that rest on stem attached to a base or foot for balance. *(not all wine glasses have stems)*

Sherry Glass – Stemware - glass that is smaller than red and white wine glasses.

The Dishware

Service plate/Charger plate – large plate sometimes used to indicate place setting at the table and acts as a base for salad plate, soup bowl and main course, usually removed before dessert.

Service plate/Charger

Bread and butter plate - small plate, placed upper left for bread, a butter knife or spreader is usually placed on the plate.

Holloware- Service ware with height and depth that is hollow in the center – water pitcher, coffee pot, teapot, creamer, sugar bowls, soup tureen etc.

Napkin Necessities:

The word napkin is derived from the French word naperon, meaning "little table cloth." Napkins, come in all sizes and textures and play a very important role, they start the meal, collect excess during the meal, and have the last touch at the end of the meal.

- ♦ Open the napkin below the table and place on lap, use it to blot mouths gently throughout the meal. Try not to wipe your face, cough into, or blow your nose with your napkin. Ladies, napkins are not for blotting lipstick.

- Napkins should not be placed around the neck, unless you are eating lobster.
- Large dinner napkins should be folded in half, the folded edge towards your knees, and the smaller napkins should be opened completely.
- Elbows, off the table when meals are being served.
- Leave the napkin on the back of, or draped over, the arm or on the seat if you have to leave the table before the end of the meal. (Put your napkin soiled side up, if you place it on the seat. (This represents to the wait staff that you will be returning to complete your meal).
- Place the napkin to the left or right of your plate at the end of the meal. (This represents for the wait staff that "I am finished.")
- When napkins are placed in rings the napkin is placed next to the fork pointed end of napkin facing the guest. After the ring is removed it should be placed to the left of the fork setting. At the end of the meal form a point with the napkin and loosely pull it through the ring, place to the left with the point facing the center of the table.
- Do not refold or crush your napkin at the end of a meal. Do not put on your plate, instead place to the left or right.

Time flies, eat dessert first, I am Crème Brûlée, Cherries Jubilee and Tiramisu what about you? ~ Author

Chapter 11

American and Continental/European Styles of Dining

There are two popular ways of how to use the knife and fork—the American style and the European or Continental style. Either is appropriate.

The American Style

In the American style, hold the knife in the right hand to cut the food, and the fork, which is holding the food in place, tines down, is in the left hand. The knife in the right is held with the index finger straight on the blunt side of the blade. The other four fingers are wrapped around the handle. After cutting a few bite size pieces of food, lay the knife across the top edge of the plate with the sharp edge of the knife facing inward. Switch the fork from the left to the right. The fork is now held like a pencil, between the index and the middle finger, except the thumb is turned up and tines of fork held upward as food is conveyed to the mouth with your fork. If you are left-handed, do the

My Etiquette Source

opposite. The fork remains throughout the meal, as it can be used, alone or with spoon or knife.

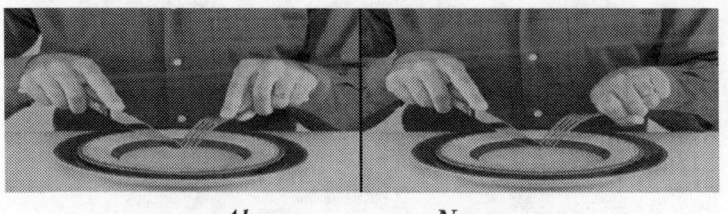

Always   *Never*

The resting position is used between bites, when blotting lips with a napkin or during conversation

"Resting American"

Knife can be rested across top of plate or along side of plate but never on the table after being used.

"I am Finished American"

The signal to the wait staff that you have completed your meal and it is time for your plate to be removed.

However, in most situations the staff often ask for permission prior to removing the plate.

"I am finished American".
(when dining with fork alone).

The European or Continental Style

Referred to as the Continental style, it is similar to the American style in that it involves cutting the food with the knife in your right hand while holding the food with the fork in your left hand. The index finger placed on the top back of the fork, while the other four fingers hold the handle of the fork. The difference? Instead of switching the fork from your left hand to your right hand, the fork remains in your left hand while the knife remains in your right hand.

Tines face *down as food is brought to your mouth.*

Resting and Closing Silverware Savvy

There are several ways to rest and close silverware. Important tip to remember: Use the "REST" position for silverware, while talking, drinking or blotting lips.

American Style of Eating Tines UP – (See page 45)

Continental or European Style of eating – Tines DOWN.

"Resting Continental Style"   *"I am Finished Continental"*

Quick Tips:

American style dining resting and closing silverware savvy:

- Resting position when only using a fork – Place the fork tines up in the plate at a 10:20 position (Basic angle)
- Resting position using knife and fork- Place the knife at the edge of the plate, blade of knife facing inside and the fork in the middle of your plate tines up. This placement works best when the plate is not full.

My Etiquette Source

- ♦ American Closing- (at the end of the meal.) Place knife and fork next to each other at the side of the plate slight angle position. Tips of the knife and fork at the top and the handles at the bottom. Tines of the fork are up. (See diagram below).

The Continental style dining resting and closing silverware savvy:

- The fork is rested on the left (tines down) and knife on the right, blade facing inward like a wide inverted "^" in the middle of your plate, the knife and fork are crossed on the plate with the tines of the fork over the knife, pointing down. (Refer to illustration on page 47).
- Continental style closing the meal – Place knife and fork next to each other on a slight angle on your plate. Like on the face of a watch or clock tips of knife and fork and handles together. Fork tines down, knife blade facing inward.

- American style tines up, Continental tines down.

Practice makes perfect you have three meals daily and there are 365 days in the year that gives you 1,095 opportunities to practice.

My Etiquette Source

Dining Etiquette – Understanding the Table Setting

Quick Tips:

When in doubt, begin with the outermost utensil and work your way toward the service plate. In other words, start from the outside and work your way in.

- ♦ It is important to place any used dishware, glassware, and utensils in the same position that they were found in order to maintain the visual presence of the table.
- ♦ Do not panic if the dessert utensils are not initially present on the table. They will be brought to you once dessert is served.
- ♦ Used plates, glassware, and utensils will be removed from the table after the conclusion of each course. Servers will remove (pick-up) from the right. Beverages are served on the right and meals on the left.
- ♦ Salad knife is optional, however, when used in Continental setting it is placed before the dinner knife.
- ♦ In most cases salad is eaten with a fork. The side of the fork is used for eating and cutting. When the salad knife is used with the salad fork its used to cut or push pieces of salad to the fork.

Salad knife is not included in settings on pages 34 and 36.

- ♦ Wine glasses are set in the order they will be used.

- Remember the rule, liquids on the right, solids on the left. "B-E-D" - bread, entree, and drink.

When all else fails follow your host/hostess or the person seated next to you.

"Private practice develops public confidence" ~ *Author*

Chapter 12

Bread, Soup, Broth/Bouillon

Bread

Now that you have familiarized yourself with the table setting, it is time to begin serving the courses of the meal. It may begin with the serving of bread. This may be in the form of a loaf of bread, bread rolls, bread sticks, flat bread, biscuits or corn bread.

- ♦ You may tear some breads by hand; rule of thumb, you break bread. Use your discretion.
- ♦ Cover loaves of bread with a napkin before handling.
- ♦ Remove bread rolls from the basket and tear. The pieces should be no larger than bite size. If spreads such as butter or jelly are provided, butter and eat before moving to the next piece.

Broth /Bouillon

Bouillon soup is a thin broth served in a bouillon cup with two handles. Service comes with a saucer and a bouillon spoon, which is smaller than a soup spoon. The broth may be sipped directly from the cup by holding both handles, or a spoon may be used. When a bouillon spoon is used it should be placed on the saucer.

Soup

Liquids with vegetables or pieces of meat are considered soups. Soups are eaten with spoons and are thicker than broth. There are two shapes of soup spoons. The round part, is referred to as the "bowl" of the spoon, which is attached to the handle. Spoons with smaller "bowls" are sometimes used for clear or lighter soups or broths. Others with larger oval "bowls" are for heavier soups.

Eating the soup - start by holding the spoon away from you, before dipping into the soup. The motion will be out, dipping into the soup bowl and bringing up to the mouth, sipping quietly from the side of the spoon.

When at rest the spoon may be positioned with its handle leaning on the edge of the bowl or on the service plate almost under the bowl, If soup is too hot, wait for it to cool do not blow on soup, nor slurp.

To get the last of the soup tilt the bowl away from you and scoop with your spoon. Do not pick up, and drink from the bowl. When finished, leave the soup spoon in the bowl or place it on the saucer or service plate.

"The disobedient fowl obeys when in a pot of hot soup."
~ Nigerian Proverb

Chapter 13

Tea, Coffee, Desserts - Cups and Saucers

Most social and professional gatherings end with tea, coffee and dessert. To avoid the usual faux pas, here are a few tips.

- Teacup or mug - place the index finger through the handle of the cup, the thumb just above it for support, and the second finger placed below the handle. The next two fingers follow the curve of the others.
- When drinking from a cup, glass or mug, do not stick out your little finger.

My Etiquette Source

- Use the cup handle, instead of cradling the cup in your hands or fingers.
- Teabags – when tea is not brewed, tea bags are used – after steeping remove with spoon and place in spare saucer, along with wrappers. When a saucer or special accoutrement is not available politely request one.
- Stirring Liquids - Stirring a cup of tea is done quietly by moving the teaspoon in a small arch back and forth in the center of the cup. Avoid touching the sides of the cup or tapping the spoon on the rim.
- After stirring remove the spoon and place it on the saucer behind the cup, with the handle of the spoon pointing in the same direction as the handle of the cup or placed in a side plate. Do not place the spoon on the saucer in front of the cup or let it drop with a loud clank.

Avoid making unnecessary clinking noises while stirring a cup or mug with a spoon or while using other cutlery during a meal. In summation, practice 'clinking noise control' when possible.

Desserts:

The dessert spoon is larger than the teaspoon and the dessert fork is smaller than the main course fork.

- ♦ Cake and pies can be eaten with a fork, unless sticky or runny use a spoon. Fork is held in the left hand and the spoon in the right hand. Use the fork to push and the spoon to eat, this is useful for cakes with lots of sticky icing, cream, and fruits such as glazed pears and peaches.

- ♦ If there are dishes with jam and cream where everyone takes a portion, each dish should have its own serving spoon.
- ♦ Never use your own utensils to dip into the jam, cream or any condiment.

"To eat is a necessity, but to eat intelligently is an art"

~Francois La Rochefoucauld

Chapter 14

Toasts

Toasts are given for many reasons, celebrations, weddings, formal and informal gatherings. There is the welcome toast – before the meal and the toast to the guest of honor after the meal. No matter the reason keep it short and simple:

- Get the attention of the guests.
- Stand, face the guest of honor or group to whom the toast is intended.
- Hold the glass, but do not raise it until the last sentence of the toast.
- State the name of the guest of honor and make the toast. Closing with - "To our guest of honor… (name)"
- Following the toast, all stand except the guest of honor and raise glasses in that direction and take a sip. (Guests may also repeat the name of the guest of honor and take a sip).
- Guests stand only for the guest of honor toast. The guest of honor remains seated and does not

sip. Responding with a nod and "Thank you". In response after the guests are seated the guest of honor stands, make a toast and take a sip.
- Informal celebratory toasts - The person making the toast can stand or remain seated if the toast is not intended for a specific person.
- You never make a toast to yourself.

"A multitude of words is no proof of a prudent mind."
~ Thales - 620BC

Chapter 15

Business Dining, Social Dining and Tipping

Business Meal – Host/Hostess

Business executives still have anxiety thinking about doing business over a meal.

Just as in real estate, it is location, location, location. It's everything in choosing a restaurant for a business meal. This is where your hosting skills really show.

- Choose a restaurant you are familiar with in service and in food.
- As the host/hostess, arrive early and choose the table.
- Secure the bill and pay ahead of time or let the server know that the bill should be given to you.

Business Meal Client or Guest

It is important to order sensibly, keeping the nature of the food in mind. For instance, it is preferred to order foods that involve the use of a fork and a knife. Avoid ordering foods that have the potential to create messes such as spaghetti, corn on the cob, lasagna, BBQ ribs, tacos, artichokes, pizza, and chicken legs. These foods should be reserved for informal dining situations.

Quick Tips:

- Arrive on time.
- Do not chew gum.
- It is very important to consider the culture of your client, and adapt accordingly.
- After a hand shake and greetings, stay focused on the matter at hand.
- Order foods that are easy to eat.
- Avoid drinking alcohol, especially during a job interview lunch or dinner.
- Avoid getting too personal.
- Discuss the next meeting if necessary, shake hands and leave the restaurant together.
- Send a Thank You note.

Informal dining rules

Most of the abovementioned apply.

Quick Tips:

- When invited remember to RSVP – Respondez s'il vous plait- (respond).
- Bring a small gift upon arrival, wine, dessert, flowers or something you think your host/hostess would appreciate.

- Do not arrive too early - preparations may still be ongoing.
- Arrive approximately 10 to 15 minutes before invited time.
- Offer assistance based upon your relationship with the host/hostess.
- Say goodbye before you leave.
- If you must go before you find the host/hostess, remind a friend to say goodbye on your behalf referred to as a "French leave". Call the next day to explain, and express your gratitude. Otherwise, a written Thank You note within 48 hours on great stationery is expected.

Restaurant Rules Business or Social

Restaurant manners are the same as manners demonstrated at home with a few changes. There are some special considerations when having a meal at a restaurant.

Quick Tips:

- If you are with a group of six or more, one of you should assume the responsibility as host. This will make it less confusing than if everyone tries to talk to the waiter or maitre de at once. This doesn't mean that this person has to pay the bill; it just gives the waiter some direction.
- If there is no waiter to seat the ladies the gentlemen should seat them (just pull out the chair and wait for them to sit and then give it a slight push).

- If someone takes you out to dinner, show some consideration for the date's wallet. It is best to order something in the middle price range.
- Should you need to call your waiter, the best way is to catch his eye and raise your hand discreetly, you may call out quietly, "Excuse me", or request a passing waiter or other restaurant staff to get his attention.
- Many times if you are dining with friends, you will go 'Dutch Treat.' This means each couple or each person will pay for themselves.
- If you have a large group, the spokesman (or host) for the group can ask for the check. The easiest way to pay it is to divide the bill according to the number of people dining and collect the same amount of money including tip from each diner. However, if there is a big difference in the cost of what members of your group ordered (one had a lobster and another had only a salad) the bill should be divided up by the cost incurred by each diner. Please try to do the divvying up as quietly and easily as possible.
- Some restaurants offer buffet lunches and dinners. When you eat at a buffet you are expected to eat all you take and leave used plates and silver on the table when you go back for seconds. The waiter should remove and replace them while you are helping yourself to the next selection.
- An average and reasonable tip is 15 to 20 percent of the bill. If your waiter has been fantastic then you can leave more.
- At the end of the meal, if touch ups are needed, use the restroom. Never comb hair at the table,

My Etiquette Source

nor place hand bags, briefcases or personal items on the table.
- As a guest - send a "Thank You" note within 24 hours. An e-mail or phone call is acceptable but a handwritten note within 48 hours is impressive. Same applies for social or informal events.

Basic Restaurant Tipping

Maitre d' or Host/Hostess	$10.00 to $20.00
Coat Attendant	$1.00 - $3.00
Bartender	15-20% of total tab or $1.00 - $3.00 per drink
Sommelier	$0. or 10 to 20% of the wine cost
Waiter/Waitress	Before tax 15 -20%
Buffet- Waiter/Waitress	Before tax 10-15%
Restroom Attendant	$1.00 - $3.00
Valet	$2.00 - $5.00
Take Out	$0. or 10% -15% if large order
Tipping Jars	$0 - $3.00
Home Delivery	10-20%

Note that tipping rates are linked to level of service.

"When dining with the enemy use a long spoon."

~ *Unknown*

Chapter 16

General Etiquette Guidelines

Table spills, elbows and everything else

Accidents happen all the time. When they do, it is good manners to handle them quickly and quietly.

Quick Tips:

- Never reach across the table, that is an accident waiting to happen.
- If you have a little food spill, scoop it up, put it back on the side of your plate. If the spill is on your clothing, dab at the stain with your napkin and some water.
- Big spill, tell the hostess immediately and offer to help clean it up (if in someone's home). Outside of the home, discreetly get the attention of the wait staff.
- Teacup spills - minimize spills by only filling three quarters of the teacup. If your tea or coffee spills

My Etiquette Source

into the saucer, request a replacement saucer. If a paper napkin is available place it under the cup to soak up the spill. Remove the wet napkin and place it on an empty plate or saucer if one is available.

- If you take a bite and get a piece of gristle, spoiled food, or a shell, simply push it to the front of your mouth with your tongue and deposit it back on your fork or spoon. Put it on the edge of your plate. Don't exaggerate or make comments.
- Never pick your teeth at the table. If you have to remove something, excuse yourself, and leave the table for a minute to resolve the problem.
- If you take a bite of something that burns your mouth, take a sip of water or milk. If you start to choke on something, try the water again. You can also cover your mouth with a napkin and try to cough or swallow. In an emergency, grab the person next to you and point to your throat.
- Do not place yours elbows on the table when food is served, forearm is acceptable before, between courses and during conversation.

General Etiquette Guidelines

Table spills, elbows and everything else

- Elbows should not be extended when using your knife and fork, keep them close to your side.
- Pocket books, briefcases, sunglasses and anything other than food, should not be placed on the table.
- Try not to play video games, read, write or use electronic devices at the table.
- When you drop a knife or fork, ask for a replacement.

"If others talk at table be attentive, but talk not with meat in your mouth." ~ George Washington

Chapter 17

Difficult Foods

Some foods are going to be awkward to eat no matter how you slice them. Here are some tips:

Fried chicken: At home or a casual dinner, you may use your fingers if your host or mother does. Take your cue from them. At a formal dinner, you should use a knife and fork.

Spaghetti: Twirl the pasta around your fork. Use a pasta spoon if one has been provided.

Rice or Grits with a fork: Hold the fork in the "pencil position" and do not overload your fork.

Corn on the cob: You may eat it with your fingers.

Pizza: You may pick it up and eat it with your fingers. It's easier and less messy to tuck in the point and fold it in half. If the pizza slice is loaded with goodies, fold or use a fork.

Melon: Eat watermelon by hand only at picnics. Otherwise, use your fork and knife or a spoon. If half a cantaloupe or melon is served, use a spoon. When fruit is served in sections, you can use a knife, fork, or spoon.

Soft shell crabs: Eat the whole thing, shell and all, with a fork and knife unless it is served in a sandwich.

Fish with bones: Remove as many bones as possible with your fork and knife. If you take a bite and find little bones, push them to the front of your mouth with as little fuss as possible, and then onto your fork. Put them on the side of your plate. This rule applies to crab cakes or anything else with shells.

Spareribs, Shish Kabob, Sandwiches and Steak: There is no easy way. You may pick them up.
Spare ribs - eat with fingers, Shish Kabob - if served as an appetizer, take small bites, eating one piece at a time. For a meal - slide meat and vegetables from skewer with fork to plate and use fork for eating.
Large sandwiches - after decorative pick is removed, eat in sections and use your fork, (if provided) to pickup excess that remains on the plate.
However, when you eat a T-bone steak, use your knife and fork to cut the meat away from the bone.

"Tell me , I will forget. Show me, I will remember. Involve me and I will understand." ~ Chinese proverb

Chapter 18

Guidelines for Confident Dining

Always

- Sit up straight; it makes a good impression.
- Keep your hands on your lap. If they must be on the table, place your wrists on the edge of the table. Elbows on the table are only acceptable between the courses of the meal, not during.
- Remember to order foods that you can eat with a knife and a fork. Foods that can create a potential mess are best left for informal dining.
- Leave the table in the event of an emergency. If you must visit the restroom or suddenly fall ill, quietly excuse yourself from the table. In the event you become ill, you may apologize to the host or hostess afterward.
- Request items to be passed to you to avoid an accident. Do not stretch across the table. If you are in need of an item that is not within easy access, politely ask the person closest to the item to hand

it to you. For example, you may say, "After you are finished, would you please pass me the salt and pepper?"
- Request items such as salt and pepper or cream and sugar together.
- Discreetly alert the attention of a waiter in the event you drop silverware on the floor or receive dirty silverware, glasses, or plates, and request a replacement.
- Invite the left-handed person to sit at the left end or head of the table. This arrangement helps to ensure everyone has adequate elbow room to eat comfortably.
- Pick up food that slips off your plate unto the table by using a piece of silverware and placing it on the edge of your plate or on a saucer. When food falls on the floor call the wait staff.
- Engage in table conversation that is pleasant but free of controversial matter.

More Guidelines for Confident Dining

Never

- In a small setting, never start eating before everyone else has received their meal. Except, in large groups you may start eating after your table or section was served.
- Never dip food in the sauce followed by a bite (chicken fingers etc) and then a repeated dip in the sauce followed by another bite – that is called double dipping It is unsanitary. If you enjoy the

dip, request a spoon and saucer and create your own dipping plate.
- Do not ask for extra servings, be considerate other guests may need to be served, sometimes others arrive late.
- Do not request a doggie bag when you are a guest. Save this for informal situations. When there is excess at informal gatherings, many host/hostess would be only too happy to share, plus it is a compliment to the cook.
- Excessive consumption of alcoholic beverages when dining out is inappropriate.
- Never smoke when dining out.
- Never season your food prior to eating.
- Do not slouch over your food, bring your food to your face and not the reverse.
- Do not chew with your mouth open and make loud noises.
- Do not talk with food in your mouth.
- Do not slurp

Thank you and Goodbye

Informal events - When leaving be sure to say "Thank you" and "goodbye" to the host. Say goodbye the way you usually do, - a hug and kiss, handshakes, sentimental parting words. Based upon the relationship, when you have arrived home, let the host/hostess be made aware by phone and thank them again for the wonderful evening.

Remember that you can thank the host/hostess by way of a hand written note, text, phone call or email.

Formal or business events, say "Thank You" with a handshake, followed by a telephone call, e-mail or text within 24 hours or a written Thank you note within forty-eight hours.

"Continually put your best foot forward and it will become a habit"

~Unknown

Chapter 19

Foreign and Other Words Found on Menus

À la carte (ah lah KAHRT) – a menu term signifying that each item is priced separately.

Aperitif- Alcoholic liqueur drink that can be taken before meals - to stimulate the appetite or after meals - digestif

Amuse-bouche (a-mooz-booSH) – French, meaning pleasing to the mouth. A complementary platter of various bite-sized tasty foods to tease the palate, sometimes served to appease customers inconvenienced by service.

Antipasto (ahn-tee-PAHS-toh) – literally meaning "before the pasta," this Italian term refers to hot or cold hors d'oeuvres.

Au jus (oh-zhoo) – a French phase describing meat served with its own juices, often used with beef.

Béarnaise sauce (behr-NAYZ) – a sauce made with a reduction of vinegar, wine, tarragon, and shallots, finished with egg yolks and butter.

Bisque (bihsk) – a thick rich soup usually of pureed seafood and cream, sometimes of vegetables or fowl.

Café (Coffee) – the very first coffee beans thought to have come from Ethiopia and found its way to Brazil and Colombia, the two largest producers of coffee today.

Crepe (KRAYP) – a thin pancake served as an entrée or dessert; a very thin creation made from plain or sweetened batters with various flours.

Croutons (KROO-tawn) – a very small piece of bread that has been browned by baking or sautéing.

Crudités (kroo-dee-TAY) – served as an appetizer, crudités are raw seasonal vegetables normally served with a dipping sauce.

Demitasse (DEHM-ee-tahss) – literally for "half cup," the term demitasse, a tiny cup used to serve coffee or very strong black coffee or espresso.

En croute (ahncroot) – baked in a pastry crust.

En papillote (AHN-pah-peeYOHT) – refers to food baked in a wrapping of parchment paper. The paper is slit open and peeled back to reveal the food.

Entrée (AHN-tray) – refers to the main course of a meal. It refers to the dish served between the fish and meat courses during formal dinners in parts of Europe.

Enchiladas – corn tortillas filled with meat and/or cheeses and topped with a chili sauce.

Éclair – oblong pastry made with dough, filled with cream, and topped with icing.

Escargot (ehs-kahr-GOH) – the French term for snail.

Filet mignon (fih-LAY-mihn-YON) – an expensive, boneless cut of beef from the small end of tenderloin.

Flambé (flahm-BAY) – French for flamed; a very dramatic food presentation of igniting certain foods after sprinkled with liquor just before serving.

French leave- Leaving an event without directly saying goodbye to the host/hostess

Fromage (froh-MAHZH) – French for cheese.

Hollandaise sauce (Hol-uhn-dayz) – a sauce of butter, egg yolks, and lemon juice used to embellish vegetables, fish, and egg dishes such as eggs Benedict.

Gumbo – a thick stock flavored with vegetables, spices, seafood, and meat of Cajun origin.

Guacamole – a dip made of avocados, cilantro, chilies, and lime, and served with chips.

Hors d'oeuvre (or DERV) – small savory appetizers served before a meal, usually one or two, bite size, and served cold or hot.

Hash browns – shredded or diced fried potatoes, sometimes meat is included.

Icing – cake toppings made with powdered sugar and butter.

Jalapeños – a variety of hot peppers, sometimes used as toppings for food.

King crab – a very large crab found in cold waters.

Kumquats – fruit resembling a very small oval orange.

Lentils – related to beans and peanuts, mostly used for soups.

Lasagna – a layered noodle dish filled with meat, cheeses, and topped with tomato sauce.

Maître d' (may-truh-DEE) – a headwaiter or house steward.

Mangoes – a tropical fruit included in some desserts.

Petit four (PEH-tee-fohr) – various bite size (frosted) iced and beautifully decorated cakes, popular at tea parties.

Quiche – a savory open-faced pastry crust filled with custard including meat and cheese.

Quesadilla – flour or corn tortilla usually filled with meat, cheeses, or vegetables.

Radish – an edible vegetable root, commonly used in salads.

RSVP – *Réspondez s'il vous plaît* is French, meaning request for responses, or let us know if you will attend.

Rice – a white or brown grain; a commonly consumed staple food.

Sorbet (sor-BAY) – French for sherbet, but is different because it contains no milk. Used as a palate refresher between meal courses or as a dessert.

Si vous plaît – French for "if you please."

Tiramisu (tirami-su) – an Italian dessert made in layers of coffee-soaked biscuits, mascarpone cheese, eggs, and sugar.

Tempura – of Japanese origin; is battered and deep-fried vegetables or seafood.

Tortillas – thin, flat bread made from wheat flour.

Udon – thick wheat noodles of Japanese origin and generally used in soups.

Ukha – a fish broth soup of Russian origin.

Veal – meat from young cattle, usually bull calf, versus beef from older cattle.

Venison – meat from deer or other game animals.

Wine – a beverage made from fermented fruit, usually grapes.

Wiri wiri peppers – a small, cherry-like variety of peppers.

Xavier souppe – a classic Italian soup.

Xacuti – an Indian dish with marinated fish or meat and spices.

Xia – Chinese for "shrimp."

Yams – a dark-skinned tuber, usually served in Caribbean soups.

Yogurt – fermented milk.

Zucchini – usually a green summer squash.

"If it is coffee, please bring me tea; but if it is tea, please bring me some coffee." ~ Abraham Lincoln

Chapter 20

My Mini Etiquette Dictionary

A

À La Carte: This means that each item on the restaurant menu is ordered and priced separately as opposed to a table d'hôte meal in which all courses are included in the price.

Abbreviations: A shortened form of a written word or phrase used in place of the whole.

Accessories: Professional, social, formal or informal - Select attire and accessories that are appropriate for the occasion.

Acknowledgment: The accepted way of acknowledging a compliment is to smile and say thank you. If you are given a gift in person, sending a thank you note is not necessary, but it is a nice thing to do, especially if you aren't a close friend of the giver. Thank you notes for gifts received through the mail should be sent within a week; not only is this the polite thing to do, but a note of thanks dashed off immediately after the gift arrival will connote an air of gratitude.

American Style of Eating (see Dining Skills)

Anniversary: The annual recurrence of a date marking a notable event. A date that follows such an event by a specified period of time measured in units other than years.

Anniversary Party: Often celebrated on the weekend nearest to the date of the anniversary, as a matter of convenience and permit out-of-town guests to travel to the party.

Announcements: At a formal luncheon or such function where there is no receiving line, the servant who has greeted the guest at the door then directs the guest into the living room, walks to within speaking distance of the hostess, and announces the guest's name.

Aperitif: A small alcoholic drink taken before a meal to stimulate the appetite, also called aperitif wine.

Appetizer: The appetizer is the first course of a meal. It may consist of a shrimp cocktail, fruit juice, hors d'oeuvre, or any food that serves to sharpen the appetite. Also used to whet and excite the palate.

Appointment: Breaking—it goes without saying that the other person or persons involved should be notified as quickly as possible. Personal engagements require an explanation, of course. It is a good idea in breaking an appointment, whether business or personal, to suggest another future time for meeting.

B

Birth Announcements: This could read "Mr. and Mrs. Eugene Jones of Rockaway, Queens NY, announce the birth of a son, Edward Anthony Jones, on April 15th in Franklin General Hospital."

Bachelor Dinner: It is traditional for the groom-to-be to give a dinner two or three nights before the wedding for the best man, ushers, and other male friends. Sometimes the fathers in the wedding party and the husbands of the bridal attendants join in the fun, too. The dinner is held either in a private dining room or in the groom's bachelor apartment. Either way, a professional caterer will probably take care of the food. This factor, plus the amount of liquor usually consumed at such dinners, will indicate just how expensive a bachelor dinner can be. The groom-to-be is the host and so, of course, arrives first.

Baptism or Christening: The christening ceremony is almost identical among all faiths who believe in baptism. Usually, godparents have been appointed and attend, especially if the child is under six or seven years old. Invitations to a christening are extended to only very close friends and relatives and are issued informally by note, telephone, or in person. The ceremony often takes place immediately following a Sunday church service, and those attending will wear their usual church-going dress. The child will dress in white.

Best Man: The best man's duties in a formal wedding are varied and somewhat trying. He will be responsible for most, if not all these chores: arranging the bachelor dinner, seeing the ushers are properly dressed, instructed in their duties, and present at the rehearsal and church at least an hour before the ceremony. He is in charge of the newlywed's luggage, either stowing it in the going-away car or forwarding the luggage to the honeymoon spot.

Beverages: Liquids other than water, as in tea, coffee, beer, milk, juices, soda, and sparkling water. Plus creative cocktails—alcoholic and nonalcoholic.

Black Tie: Dress code for social functions, including evening events.

Bon Voyage A French word for have a good trip (safe, nice, etc).

Boutonniere (bou-ton-niere): a flower worn in a buttonhole.

Brandy: Served after dinner, usually with coffee. Brandy is poured into a brandy snifter, a glass designed to let the drinker warm the brandy with his hands as he drinks it.

Bread and Butter (see Dining)

Bridal Registry: As soon as a woman knows she is going to be married, she may go to her local department store or specialty house wares store and register her gift preferences.

Bridal Shower: Any close friend or relative of the bride may give a shower for her, but members of the immediate bride or groom may not. Showers are usually informal

My Etiquette Source

affairs—invitations are issued and accepted via informal note or telephone. Everyone attending a shower should bring a gift, usually inexpensive and practical since most of the guests will give the bride and groom a present later. The verbal thank you from the bride at the shower is sufficient.

Bride: The bride's responsibilities are to plan her wedding and look her loveliest on her wedding day.

Bridegroom: If the wedding is a large and formal one, with the bride in full regalia it is essential other members of the wedding party dress accordingly.

Bridesmaid: Female attendant at a wedding who assists the bride.

Brunch: Meal that combines breakfast and lunch and generally eaten late in the morning.

Buffet: Meal at which people serve themselves from various dishes set out on a serving counter or table.

Business Apparel: Business clothing appropriate for the corporate world as in suits, ties, and dresses.

Business Entertaining: Free or subsidized entertainment or hospitality designed for clients and/or employees.

Business Etiquette: Guidelines and protocols for acceptable behavior. Start by using the golden rule treating others the way you would like to be treated in a professional or social setting.

Butter Plate: Butter plates are always placed above the forks to the left of the dinner plate. The butter and butter knife should be in place when the diner sits down at the table. There are several ways the knife may be placed. The most common is across the top of the plate, blade toward the user, and the handle to his right.

C

Cake: Cakes are often served on joyful events such as birthdays, anniversaries, and showers. After the bride, the centerpiece at weddings is where the most elaborate and beautiful cakes are seen.

Canapé (see Appetizer): Small, decorative pieces of bread topped with a savory garnish such as anchovy, cheese, or some type of spread. Crackers or pastry may also be used as a base. Canapés may be simple or elaborate, hot or cold. They are usually served as an appetizer with cocktails. The word canapé is French for couch.

Caterer: Person hired to prepare the food at a party.

Caviar: This expensive appetizer is simply sieved and lightly salted fish roe (eggs). Sturgeon roe is premium and considered true caviar. The three main types of caviar are Beluga, Osetra, and Sevruga. The best is from the Beluga sturgeons that swim in the Caspian Sea bordered by Russia and Iran. Caviar production is a major industry for both countries.

Champagne: The most celebrated sparkling wine always seems to signal special occasions. There are two kinds

My Etiquette Source

of champagne—golden and champagne rosé—the latter being rare. Champagne can be dry (brut), semi dry, or sweet. Dry champagne should be served ice cold or only slightly chilled. Champagne is appropriate on just about any occasion with the possible exception of an informal luncheon. Opinion is divided on whether champagne should be served ice cold or only slightly chilled. At any rate, drink it as soon as you open the bottle, as it will go flat in a matter of moments.

Christening: Religious practice involving the church and clergyman (minister or pastor).

Cocktail Buffet: Finger food provided at a social setting or a buffet where you serve yourself or with some assistance.

Cocktail Party: An evening gathering.

Coffee: A beverage from coffee beans.

Consommé: A very light or thin soup made from stock.

Continental Style of Eating (see Dining)

Corsage: Small bouquet of flowers worn on women's dresses or on the wrist for weddings, graduations, proms, and special parties such as a "sweet sixteen" party.

Cotillion: Social gathering for dancing where young women are formally introduced to society and young men may meet their future wives.

Cummerbund: A sash, usually pleated and brightly colored, worn by men as part of a formal dress.

D

Debutante Ball: A formal ball where people are introduced to society.

Dinner Jacket (see Black Tie): An evening suit or a tuxedo, usually black and worn with formal pants, shirt, tie, and accessories as the event demands.

Dinner: Formal—a formal dinner is usually after 7:00 p.m. and is a heavier meal than supper. A host/hostess and guest of honor, usually four- to six-course meal. The host enters with the guest of honor followed by couples. The hostess enters last and accompanies the most important man. The host sits at one end of the table and the hostess at the other end. **Informal**—at an informal dinner, the hostess enters followed by the women guests and then the men. Guests stand behind their chairs until the hostess starts to take her seat, and then they are seated.

E

Eggcup: Decorative container used for serving cooked eggs.

Etiquette: Social rules and guidelines.

Escargot: The French term for "snail."

Expense Accounts: Funds allotted to employees or individuals usually on business trips.

F

Finger Bowl: Small bowl with water placed on the dining table for dipping fingers after a meal. Dry your fingers with a napkin.

Finger Food (see Buffet, Cocktail Party): Tasty morsels eaten with fingers or a small fork.

Flatware (see Table Manners)

Forks (see Flatware)

G

Garden Parties: Today the term has come to mean simply an informal tea held in a garden or patio. The food served is light and dress is informal. A woman would wear cotton or linen dress and a hat; men would wear a lightweight suit and hat.

Garnish: To add something as an accompaniment to food or drink that enhances its flavor or appearance.

Gifts: Something given to somebody to provide pleasure or show gratitude.

Glassware: Glasses at a formal dinner table need not all be alike, but they should look well together. However, all wine glasses should match. All glasses required throughout the meal are in place at the beginning of the dinner and placed in order of their use. They are placed to the right above the knives. Each glass is removed with the course it accompanied with the exception of the dessert wine glass that remains so long as guests are seated.

Gloves: It is not necessary to remove your gloves when shaking hands outdoors, however; when indoors, they should be removed.

Golf: At the first tee, there are no rules governing the matter of the precedence; women and guest are usually given the first drive. Thereafter, it's the winner of the previous hole who drives first.

Gossip: Avoid at all costs. If you cannot say something positive, be silent.

Grace: A moment of silence at the beginning of the meal for the family to say a blessing.

Graduation: Completion of required courses or training.

Greeting (see Introductions)

Guest of Honor: A special guest usually seated to the right of the host/hostess.

H

Handshakes (see Introduction)

Handwriting: Take your time, be legible, and be considerate because someone other than yourself may have to read it.

Honeymoon: A short period of harmony or goodwill at the beginning of a relationship.

Hors d'oeuvres (see Foods)

Host/Hostess: Someone responsible for ensuring guests enjoy themselves while accepting their hospitably. Guests are welcomed, shown to their seats, and introductions made as needed.

Hotels: Buildings or commercial establishments where people pay for lodging and where meals and other facilities such as conference rooms are often available.

Checking In: Actual process of getting into a hotel

Checking Out: Process for leaving the hotel

I

Intermission: A break between parts of a musical or theatrical performance or in the showing of a movie in a movie theater.

Introduction: The act of formally presenting somebody or yourself to another person in order to make that person's acquaintance.

Invitation: An offer to come or go somewhere, especially one promising pleasure or hospitality, or the making of such an offer.

J

Junior: Abbreviation is "Jr." Used to distinguish a son from his father when they have the same given name. It's also used to identify younger or lower in rank and size.

Jokes: Those that seem funny in one culture can be offensive to or misinterpreted by someone from another culture.

Justice (address): Honorable Judge or Chief Justice.

K

Kissing: Display of affection to touch or caress with the lips as an expression of love, greeting, and respect. Glamour kisses are not touching, but gesturing on each side of the cheek. A peck is a gentle touch of the cheek. Hand kissing is a gesture indicating courtesy, politeness, respect, and admiration. A male hand is extended to a female, palm up making strong eye contact, and a single kiss is placed on the back of the hand.

Kiss: A small piece of chocolate candy or a cookie made of egg whites and sugar.

Kumquats: Oval-shaped, orange-like fruit the size of a bird's egg.

L

Letter of Introduction: Reference letter from a company or friend.

Liquor: A distilled alcoholic beverage sometimes used as a base ingredient for the production of liqueur.

Liqueur: Infuses flavoring agents and has added sugar syrup. Liqueur has a weaker alcoholic proof than liquor. Both fall under the category of spirits.

Luggage: Are suitcases, bags, and other items for carrying personal belongings during a journey.

Lunch: Meal around noon (informal) or a **Luncheon** (formal).

M

Madam: Used to address a woman, a polite term of address for a woman, especially a customer in a store, restaurant, or hotel. It is synonymous with "ma'am" or "Mrs."

Maid of Honor: Traditionally, the maid of honor is the unmarried best friend or sister of the bride.

Matron of Honor: The matron of honor is usually a close friend or relative of the bride who is married. These women stand to the left of the bride during the wedding ceremony. Their duties are mainly to assist with the wedding planning and helping the bride get ready on her wedding day. They also plan the bridal shower.

Maiden Name: A woman's surname before marriage.

Minister: Usually a clergyman, but also used for government cabinet members.

N

Name Plates: Means of identification, worn on the upper right side of a garment.

Napkin (see Dining Skills)

O

Obituary: An announcement, especially in a newspaper of somebody's death and often includes a short biography.

Obscenities: Are inappropriate or vulgar language or behavior.

Office Etiquette: Acceptable and respectful behavior in business setting.

Office Party: An event for all levels of employees and business associates where applicable.

Open House: Is by public invitation.

P

Party: A gathering of people for a celebration.

Passing Food: When food is served family-style, it is passed around among the diners so each person may help herself or himself.

Paying: Reward for service.

Place Cards: Place cards are used at any dinner where the host/hostess wants or needs a plan for seating their guests.

Place Setting: (see Dishes, Fork, Knife, Napkin, and Spoon)

Prejudice: Unfavorable opinion based on lack of knowledge, irrational feelings, and misconceptions of an individual or thing. Usually based on religion, ethnicity, nationality, or social status.

Prix fixe: A prix fixe menu is one in which the price is preset or fixed for the meal served.

Profanity: Vulgar language.

Q

Queen's English: A grammatically correct written expression of the English language.

Quiche: A savory pie filled with an egg-and-cream mixture and various meats or vegetable ingredients.

Queue: A line of people waiting to gain entrance for transportation or events.

R

Respect: The foundation of good manners on display for yourself and others.

Receiving Line: Used for some formal affairs such as weddings and special events. The purpose of a receiving line is to allow the host or hostess to welcome guests. At formal events, names of guests are announced upon arrival. At weddings, this is usually done at the reception site. When the receiving line is not used at weddings, the bride and groom should visit each table.

Traditional etiquette dictates receiving lines are made up of the following:

Mother of the bride, Mother of the groom, Bride, Groom, Maid of honor All the bridesmaids

This may be shortened to include:

Mother of the bride, Father of the groom, Bride and groom, Mother of the groom

Father of the bride

Reception: Formal or informal gathering to welcome somebody or celebrate an event such as a wedding, state, or professional affair usually held at home or in a public space. This could vary from celebratory gatherings, refreshments, and dining and dancing to a more relaxed event.

RSVP: *Répondez s'il vous plaît*; French for request for responses or reply if you please.

S

Seating arrangement: The orderly provision of seats that would benefit the outcome of an event, school, auditorium, church, public, or private gathering.

Secretary: An employee who does clerical and administrative work in an office for a person or an organization.

Servants: An employee who serves somebody else, especially an employee hired to do household tasks or acts as a personal attendant.

Sorbet: A palate cleanser between meals.

Si Vous Plaît: French for "if you please."

Slipping: Discretely mention the word slipping to notify a woman when her slip or bra strap is showing.

Squid: The edible parts of the squid include the arms (tentacles), the mantle (tube), and the fins (wings). The body is covered with a thin skin that may be removed before cooking. Squid ink is often used to make black pasta.

Sommelier: Trained wine expert.

Stationery: Paper used for writing letters or other forms of correspondence.

Supper: A light evening meal usually before dinner.

Table d'hôte: Table d'hôte is French for the host/hostess table. A table assigned for customers or guests; the same table as their host. For restaurants, this refers to a menu with several meals where a few items are charged at a fixed price.

Table Manners: Special guidelines for appropriate behavior while dining.

Table setting: The orderly presentation of cutlery, china and stemware. (see pages 34 and 36)

Telephone Etiquette: Guidelines for appropriate telephone greetings and conversations over the phone.

Theater: A building, room, or other setting where plays or other dramatic presentations are performed.

Tipping: Guidelines to reward for service.

Tuxedo (see Black Tie): Formal men's attire.

U

Usher: Someone who escorts people to their seats in a place such as a theater or a church.

My Etiquette Source

Urinal Etiquette/Restroom: At home or away from home, pay strict attention to cleanliness and hygiene. Remember to tip the attendant.

V

Visiting Cards (see Business Cards)

W

Workplace Etiquette: People should always conduct themselves in a professional manner using some of the basic manners and etiquette skills.

Waiter/Waitress: Usually servers at dining events or restaurants.

Wedding: A ceremony in which two people get married.

Weekend Guests: Guest(s) who stay for no more than three days.

Wine: Usually made from fermented grapes or other fruits in various colors: red, white, and pink. There are special glasses for different wines, and the wine expert is called a sommelier.

Women's Social Titles: Miss, Mrs., Ms. Madam, Dame, Countess, First Lady, Gentlewoman, Congresswoman, Queen, Princess.

X

XYZ or XYZPDQ: e*X*amine *Y*our *Z*ipper. Quietly mention *XYZ* or *XYZPDQ* to notify someone if a zipper is open on a pair of pants.

Y

Yearbook: A permanent record of an event. Remember when you pose for photographs. Avoid gimmicks and racy fashion trends. Go for the classic look and style.

Z

Zig Zag: American dining style that begins with the knife in the right hand and the fork in the left hand. Cut the meat and then switch the fork to the right for dining. The knife remains in the resting position across the top edge of the plate with the blade facing toward you.

"Let food be your medicine" ~ *Hippocrates*

Notes

About Us

Trudy and I met during a certification program sponsored by the Protocol School of Washington. Trudy was an international flight attendant, and at the time, I was an aviation financial analyst. Trudy is a Southern Belle with an international flare, and I have a British /Caribbean upbringing. I am currently working and living in New York. We make quite a team.

One year following the completion of my certification, I was able to successfully transition to a new career path in aviation customer service as a full-time profession while developing and growing the Etiquette & Protocol Centre. There are currently offices in New York and Arkansas, so it is quite clear that Trudy and I are still working together.

We are in the people business, and we realize the need to bridge the gap between the academic and business world. We love to help and serve. While we cannot do much to help everyone financially, our best is to provide enough information to improve awareness to help you have a successful life.

Notes

About the Authors

Cheryl Lee is the director of the Etiquette Centre of Long Island. The centre is committed to helping individuals develop and enhance skills necessary to thrive and excel in today's professional and social environment. Her passion for education through enrichment programs and seminars has inspired her to develop The Competitive Connection, a program uniquely designed to bridge the gap between the academic and business world.

Ms. Lee presents etiquette and customer service programs nationwide geared to entertain, educate, and motivate individuals to outclass the competition. She is a certified corporate etiquette and international protocol consultant trained at the prestigious Protocol School of Washington. (This is the first company in the United States to provide professional training and certification in etiquette and international protocol.) Other credentials include an MBA in corporate finance from Long Island University and a BBA in general business from Pace University. Ms. Lee has more than thirty years of business experience that includes financial analysis, business education, customer service, airport operations, and transportation.

Trudy Redus is the founder and director of The Protocol School of Arkansas - The Etiquette Solution. She later partnered with EPCLI (Etiquette & Protocol Centre of Long Island) and that alliance created The Etiquette & Protocol Centre of Arkansas and Long Island, NY. She is a graduate of The Protocol School of Washington.® Under the direction of Dorothea Johnson, one of the first schools in the country to offer training and certification to teach business etiquette and international protocol.

Trudy received a B.S. degree from North Carolina A&T State University and an AA Culinary Arts from the Art Institute of Atlanta. She continues to work with colleges and universities throughout the country with a program she developed called "Graduating a Class Ahead. ®" These programs are designed to provide college students the assurance and self-confidence needed to be successful in life.

Throughout the year she has programs for teens and young adults, in addition to a summer camp for children called "Mini Manners." She offers a series of workshops and seminars in various cities for targeted audiences and the general public.

About the Book

The book is designed to be your etiquette source. That is why there is an opening on the cover for you to insert your photograph or that of the person for whom the book was purchased. If the book was purchased as a graduation gift, insert the photograph of the graduate or a photograph of the one with the special birthday or occasion.

There are definitions and famous quotes, words of encouragement, room for notes, special clips, or articles that the owner may wish to collect and use as a reference to enhance his or her skills. This book does not end with the author, but with you, the reader, keeping this work alive as you enjoy your personal journey.

Thank you Joyce - for your encouragement
Thank you Jerry - Photographer
and Amanda - Model

Thank you

The Etiquette and Protocol Center would like to thank the following organizations, schools and colleges for allowing us to bring our vision to their establishment:

Boys and Girls Club of Suffolk County- NY
Mentoring Moms
Mocha Moms
Elmont Elementary School District
Elmont Memorial Public Library
Northport High School
Freeport Public Library
Locust Valley Public Library
Baruch College – New York
Farmingdale College
Philander Smith College – Little Rock, Arkansas
University of Arkansas – Pine Bluff
Pace University
Pathways to Empowerment- Queens NY
Pine Bluff Chamber of Commerce – Leadership Program
Financial Women Association
Montefiore Hospital Centers
Summer Camp – I Rock - AR
Summer Camp – Technology meets Civility

"As iron sharpens iron so man sharpens another."
~ Proverbs 27:17

Notes

Notes

Notes

Notes

Notes